TO OUR MOTHERS, DEB & CHRIS,
WHO INSTILLED IN BOTH OF US A LOVE
FOR PLANTS AT AN EARLY AGE,
AND WHO BOTH LEFT US FAR TOO SOON.

CONTENTS

SUCCULENTS

An Illustrated
FIELD GUIDE

by Kit Carlson, PhD, and Aaron Carlson

illustrated by Vlad Stankovic

13-Digit ISBN: 978-1-64643-453-4
10-Digit ISBN: 1-64643-453-6

This book may be ordered by mail from the publisher. Please include $5.99
for postage and handling. Please support your local bookseller first!

Books published by Cider Mill Press Book Publishers are available at special
discounts for bulk purchases in the United States by corporations, institutions, and
other organizations. For more information, please contact the publisher.

Cider Mill Press Book Publishers
"Where good books are ready for press"
501 Nelson Place
Nashville, Tennessee 37214
cidermillpress.com

Cover and interior design by Melissa Gerber
Typography: Adobe Caslon, Caslon 540, DIN 2014, Eveleth
Clean Thin, Fontbox Boathouse Filled

Printed in Malaysia

23 24 25 26 27 OFF 5 4 3 2 1

First Edition

INTRODUCTION

THE EVOLUTIONARY ORIGINS OF SUCCULENTS

Imagine that we are "time-traveling horticulturalists," and we want to learn what might have happened to common garden seeds like peas or beans if we had tried to cultivate them on Earth a billion years ago. Traveling back in time, we would encounter a planet covered by vast oceans and barren, rocky lands. The weathered rock and sediment on the land surfaces would contain little organic material. The atmosphere would contain toxic gases like methane, carbon monoxide, and ammonia but almost no oxygen. The ozone layer would be thin or nonexistent, and the ultraviolet radiation striking the land's surface would be at least 100 times more intense than it is today. Modern-day plants like peas and beans have evolved through millions of years of natural selection to adapt to current Earth conditions and would be very unlikely to survive in such a vastly different environment.

During this ancient period, known as the Neoproterozoic Era, life was restricted to aquatic environments due to the intense ultraviolet radiation that would kill living cells on land. However, the changes in our planet's geology and climate that unfolded during this fascinating time period set the stage for the Cambrian explosion, occurring around 541 to 520 million years ago when our fossil records document a dazzling array of new life forms. Despite this rapid diversification of life on Earth, including most major animal groups making their grand entrance onto the scene, life was still restricted to aquatic environments.

Shortly after the Cambrian explosion, we see the ancient precursors of plants begin their transition to land. These photosynthetic organisms adapted to live at the water's edge and gradually expanded their habitat further from the shoreline. They developed various adaptations to thrive in the terrestrial environment that offered abundant sunlight for growth and no competition for space and resources.

Many cellular and molecular features characteristic of modern land plants emerged during this crucial time, enabling plants to colonize Earth's once barren landscape. The earliest adaptation in land plants is the presence of a waxy coating called a cuticle layer. This coating helps prevent the plant from drying out when not submerged in water. Next observed in the fossil record is vascular tissue. These specialized structures, called xylem and phloem, transport water and sugar throughout the plant body. Over the span of millions of years, plants became decreasingly dependent on water for reproduction as pollen emerged on the evolutionary scene, thus creating a mechanism to transport sperm that does not require the sperm to swim through a film of water. Finally, the emergence of flowers, fruits, and seeds about 100 million years ago has resulted in a tremendous diversity of plants, including countless fascinating mechanisms for successful reproduction, dispersal, and survival.

Over time, as land plants diversified and transformed both the atmosphere and the land, they also evolved specific characteristics that helped them survive and thrive in various climate regimes around the globe, leading to the variety of plant life on Earth today. For example, plants in areas with high rainfall, such as rainforests, have adapted to nutrient-leached soil due to excessive precipitation. As a result, these rainforest plant species may have shallow root systems to absorb nutrients from decaying leaves and tend to grow quickly and vertically to maximize sunlight exposure. Rainforest plants also have leaves with pointed tips to facilitate water dripping off the surface, preventing potential bacterial or fungal infections.

The adaptations observed in each species match the climatic conditions of the area. Cold-tolerant plants can withstand freezing temperatures by moving water out of their cells to prevent the cell from bursting when frozen, or produce antifreeze compounds to prevent the cell from freezing. Many plants also undergo senescence or dormancy, shedding their leaves and entering a dormant state during cold periods. Structural adaptations, such as downward-sweeping branches of conifer trees, also evolved to deal with snow accumulation. Plant species that evolved in arid environments such as deserts, tundras, chaparrals, or salt flats developed various strategies to survive in dry conditions.

The focus of this book is on another adaptation that has evolved in plants that inhabit dry areas, and that is succulence. Succulent plants have developed specialized cells and tissues that store water. These specialized water storage tissues may occur in the succulent plant's leaves, stem, and roots, often imparting a swollen or fleshy appearance to the plant.

The cacti are probably the most well-known group of succulent plants. All cacti have evolved to store water in specialized stem tissue. Regardless of the size or shape of a cactus, the stem makes up most of the plant body. For example, although they are quite distinctive in appearance, the flat pads of the prickly pear and the long, tall spires of a saguaro are both comprised of specialized stem tissues. The spines on cacti are modified leaves that have evolved to minimize water loss, prevent herbivory, provide shade, and direct raindrops down toward the base of the plant, similarly to how pointed leaf tips help shed water off the surface of leaves in wet climates.

Other dry-climate adaptations will vary by species. For example, some succulents may have deep taproot systems, extra-thick waxy coatings on their leaves, or pubescence to minimize water loss. Some succulent plants shed their leaves and go dormant during dry periods, while others have smaller or reduced leaves to limit transpiration.

Succulent species also often have unique pollination and flowering strategies, demonstrating the complex interactions between the plant and its environment. For example, many succulent species produce very fragrant flowers. This is likely because fragrance is especially useful in hot, sunny climates where the fragrance molecules will quickly volatilize and spread rapidly to attract pollinators. Some succulent species, including many cacti and some *Echeveria*, bloom at night to attract nocturnal pollinators like bats and moths. Night-blooming plants often have white or pale-colored flowers to stand out in the dark and may also release strong scents to attract pollinators. Some succulent plants have developed unique floral structures to facilitate pollination. For example, *Orbea* has flowers that mimic rotting meat in appearance and odor to attract carrion flies for pollination. The long tubular flowers of *Agave* are adapted for pollination by bats or hummingbirds.

THE CARE AND CULTIVATION OF SUCCULENTS

Most of the succulents included in this book are relatively low-maintenance and will thrive with proper care. All succulents are adapted to thrive in arid climates. However, not all dry climates are the same. Latitude and altitude are significant factors that influence the properties of arid regions. For example, scorching hot deserts like the Sahara near the equator can exceed 110°F (43°C) in the summer months, and frigid deserts, like the Gobi, located farther north of the equator, can drop as low as -22°F (-30°C) in the winter!

Each arid climate type supports different plant and animal species uniquely adapted to these conditions. The variations in temperature, precipitation, and seasonality shape the ecosystems and biodiversity within these diverse arid environments. These variations should be considered when developing a plan to care for and cultivate a specific succulent species.

BASIC CARE CONSIDERATIONS

SOIL: Succulents require well-draining soil that mimics a naturally arid environment. Use a succulent or cactus soil mix, or create your own by combining potting soil with perlite, sand, or pumice in a 1:1 ratio.

WATERING: Succulents require less frequent watering than other plants. Soil should dry between waterings, then be watered thoroughly from the bottom of the pot. Reduce watering frequency during the winter months as succulents enter a dormant period.

LIGHT: Succulents require bright, indirect light for optimal growth. Most succulents need at least six hours of sunlight per day. Rotate plants weekly to ensure even growth.

TEMPERATURE: Most succulents grow best in the temperature range between 60°F–85°F (15°C–30°C). Some can tolerate cooler temperatures during the winter, but most cannot survive a freeze. Succulents that can survive freezing should not receive any watering during very cold or freezing conditions, as this will almost always kill your plant.

FERTILIZING: Succulents do not require frequent fertilization, but a very light application of a water-soluble fertilizer during the growing season (spring and summer) can promote healthy growth Use a fertilizer formulated for succulents or cacti, and follow the manufacturer's instructions.

REPOTTING: Repot succulents every two to three years or when they outgrow their current container. Remove the plant from its pot, trim any dead or damaged roots, and place it in a new container with fresh, well-draining soil. Wait a few days before watering to allow the roots to recover and prevent root rot.

PEST CONTROL: Succulents may occasionally attract pests such as mealybugs, aphids, or spider mites. Inspect your plants regularly; if you observe pests, treat infested areas with insecticidal soap, neem oil, or a diluted rubbing alcohol solution.

CULTIVATION

Stem and leaf cuttings are frequently used to propagate succulents. Stem cuttings can be made by cutting a healthy 5 to 10 cm–long stem section with leaves or leaf nodes. To prevent rot, remove the lower leaves and place the cutting in water or well-draining soil, ensuring it stays moist and receives bright, indirect light. After two to four weeks, roots will begin to develop from the bottom, and new shoot growth will occur at the top, eventually forming a new plant identical to the parent.

Leaf cuttings can be made by carefully and gently twisting the leaf to remove it from the stem, keeping the entire leaf intact. Allow leaves to sit in a cool, dry location for several days to allow a callus to form. Place the callused portion of the leaf in well-drained soil and water just enough to prevent the leaves and new roots from drying out.

Succulents often produce offsets, or "pups," around the base of the parent plant, taking advantage of their adaptation to store water and nutrients. To propagate through offsets, gently separate the pup from the parent, ensuring it has some roots attached. Plant the pup in well-draining soil and water sparingly until it establishes a more robust root system.

Seed germination for succulents, although challenging, is another cultivation strategy influenced by their unique adaptations. Germination times can vary widely depending on the succulent species. Before attempting to germinate succulent seeds, you must determine if the succulent species requires specific seed preparation techniques, such as cold stratification. After appropriate seed preparation, fill a pot with a well-draining soil mix containing sand or perlite to mimic their natural habitat, then sprinkle the seeds on top. Lightly cover the seeds with sand and maintain moist but not wet conditions. Pots should be placed in a bright, warm location.

AIZOACEAE

Astridia	*Ebracteola*	*Monilaria*
Braunsia	*Fenestraria*	*Nananthus*
Cheiridopsis	*Frithia*	*Neohenricia*
Delosperma	*Lapidaria*	*Oscularia*
Dinteranthus	*Lithops*	*Titanopsis*

A large family of about 130 genera and at least 1,800 species. They are commonly referred to as fig marigolds, ice plants, carpet weeds, vygies, and mesembs, among many other names. More than ninety-five percent of the species are native to South Africa, with the remainder native to Australia and other Pacific islands. Most species are herbaceous annuals or perennials, with a few shrubs and tree species. Most, if not all, species are considered succulent, with thick fleshy leaves that rarely have teeth, tubercules, or other types of projections. Their flowers are either solitary or produced in cymes. They are generally five-parted and lack petals, although many have petal-like structures derived from staminodes. It is one of the younger families of flowering plants, having emerged between 1.5 and 6 million years ago.

ICE PLANT

COMMON NAME(S)
Ice Plant

SCIENTIFIC NAME
Astridia velutina

GENUS ETYMOLOGY: Honors Astrid Schwantes (1887–1960), wife of German botanist Gustav Schwantes.

SPECIES ETYMOLOGY: From the Latin word for "fleece" (*vellus*).

CORE CHARACTERISTICS: A small, mat-forming subshrub up to 20 cm tall, with fleshy, three-angled leaves that superficially resemble a boat. The leaves are grayish green with a paler margin, up to 4 cm long and 1 cm wide. The flowers are daisy-like and white with numerous long, thin petals, with an overall diameter of up to 4 cm. They are opposite in arrangement, with each pair perpendicular to the pair above and below.

ORIGIN AND HABITAT: It is native to Namibia and occurs in dry, shrubby deserts.

BEADS LAMPRANTHUS

COMMON NAME(S)
Beads Lampranthus

SCIENTIFIC NAME
Braunsia maximiliani

GENUS ETYMOLOGY: In honor of Ferdinand Braun (1850–1918), a German scientist.

SPECIES ETYMOLOGY: In honor of Maximilian zu Wied-Neuwied (1782–1867), a German naturalist.

CORE CHARACTERISTICS: A compact perennial shrublet with creeping or trailing branches up to 20 cm long. The leaves are oppositely arranged, with each pair partially fused at their base. Each leaf is three-angled and boat-shaped, up to 10 mm long, and 6–8 mm thick. They are primarily grayish green in color and papillate over nearly the entire surface. Flowers are solitary, borne terminally on a stalk that rises slightly above the leaves. They are daisy-like in appearance, up to 25 mm in diameter, with numerous pink petals.

ORIGIN AND HABITAT: It is native to the Western Cape and Northern Cape provinces of South Africa, where it grows on mossy, shallow pans on bare rock.

LOBSTER CLAWS

COMMON NAME(S)
Lobster Claws,
Carpet Weed

SCIENTIFIC NAME
Cheiridopsis denticulata

GENUS ETYMOLOGY: From the Greek words for "sleeve" and "resembling" (*cheiris* and *opsis*), in reference to the shape of its dead leaves, which sheath the emerging leaves.

SPECIES ETYMOLOGY: From the Latin word for "having teeth" (*denticulatus*).

CORE CHARACTERISTICS: A small, cushion-forming perennial plant that grows to about 10 cm tall and 30 cm wide. It has grayish-white leaves arranged in opposite pairs on short, ground-level branches. The leaves are triangular in cross section and have a slightly wrinkled surface, especially during extended dry periods. They are up to 6.5 cm long and 1 cm broad, with each pair of leaves often unequal in size and partially fused at their bases. The flowers are up to 8 cm in diameter and are cream to pale yellow or orange, occasionally with purplish-red tips.

ORIGIN AND HABITAT: It is native from South Africa to southern Namibia, where it can be found in open, dry areas, such as dry riverbeds and exposed bedrock. It often grows in dense colonies, with no other plant species present.

ICE PLANT

COMMON NAME(S)
Ice Plant

SCIENTIFIC NAME
Delosperma lehmannii
(syn. *Corpuscularia*
lehmannii)

GENUS ETYMOLOGY: From the Greek words for "visible" and "seed" (*delos* and *sperma*).

SPECIES ETYMOLOGY: Honors German botanist Johann Georg Christian Lehmann (1792–1860).

CORE CHARACTERISTICS: A compact, cushion-forming perennial, reaching 20 cm tall and 30 cm wide. It produces numerous short, sprawling branches that are densely packed with opposite pairs of nearly imbricate leaves. The leaves are ovate to globose in shape, up to 16 mm long and 8 mm wide. They are bluish green. Flowering stems are erect, bearing three-angled keeled leaves up to 4 cm long and 10 mm wide, more distantly spaced apart than the branch leaves. Inflorescences are borne at the end of these stems in a many-flowered cyme. The flowers are about 4 cm in diameter, with numerous translucent staminodes that look like petals, ranging from white to yellow. It develops a taproot and adventitious roots that emerge from the sprawling stems.

ORIGIN AND HABITAT: It is native to the Eastern Cape province of South Africa and grows on quartzite outcrops. It is gravely endangered, primarily due to habitat loss, with only two known populations currently in existence.

STONE PLANT

COMMON NAME(S)
Stone Plant,
Pebble Plant

SCIENTIFIC NAME
Dinteranthus vanzylii

GENUS ETYMOLOGY: In honor of German botanist Gottfried Wilhelm Johannes Dinter (1868–1945).

SPECIES ETYMOLOGY: In honor of South African botanist Gert H. van Zijl (birth and death dates unknown).

CORE CHARACTERISTICS: One of the "living stone" plants, consisting primarily of a mostly-buried pair of thick leaves up to 4 cm long, either growing as solitary plants or in clusters of multiple plants. The leaves are fused, save for a small cleft at the surface. The leaf tips are broad and flattened parallel to the ground surface, appearing like a flat, river-polished stone. They are primarily whitish or grayish, marked by small reddish-brown dots that often merge into irregularly shaped lines. Extending beneath the pair of leaves is a thickened taproot. Flowers are solitary, on a short, thick stalk that emerges from the cleft between the two leaves. They are 30–40 mm in diameter, with numerous yellow to orange strap-shaped, petal-like structures derived from staminodes.

ORIGIN AND HABITAT: It is native to the Cape Province of South Africa and grows in sand and gravel deposits between larger stones.

PRINCE ALBERT VYGIE

COMMON NAME(S)
Prince Albert Vygie

SCIENTIFIC NAME
Ebracteola wilmaniae

GENUS ETYMOLOGY: From the Latin word for "without" and "bracteole" (*e* and *bracteolae*), although the plant does indeed have bracteoles.

SPECIES ETYMOLOGY: In honor of South African geologist and botanist Maria Wilman (1867–1957).

CORE CHARACTERISTICS: A compact, many-branched, and slow-growing plant that forms dense mats over time. The leaves are fleshy, three-angled (trigonus), and ensiform in shape. They are up to 2 cm long and 0.5 cm wide, and have a bluish-green color. They are arranged in slightly overlapping pairs, with only a few new leaves produced yearly. The plant grows from a thick caudex that is elevated above the soil surface. The inflorescence is a one- to three-flowered cyme that emerges from the branch tips. The flowers are 20–30 mm in diameter, with numerous strap-shaped, petal-like structures derived from staminodes. The color is usually all-white but may be pink, fading to white near the base.

ORIGIN AND HABITAT: It is native to South Africa, known from only a few sites in the Northern Cape and Free State provinces. It inhabits grassy areas in gravelly soils and grows directly on exposed sandstone rocks.

BABY TOES

COMMON NAME(S)
Baby Toes,
Window Plant

SCIENTIFIC NAME
*Fenestraria
rhopalophylla*

GENUS ETYMOLOGY: From the Latin word for "window" (*fenestra*).

SPECIES ETYMOLOGY: From the Greek words for "club-shaped" and "leaf" (*rhopalon* and *phyllon*).

CORE CHARACTERISTICS: An evergreen, mat-forming perennial that tends to remain at least partially buried, with just the upper portions of the leaves emerging above ground, forming a cluster up to 8 cm in diameter. This strategy helps the plant conserve water by limiting plant tissue exposure to the sun and remaining hidden from potential herbivores. The leaves are up to 4 cm long and are fleshy and club-shaped with a waxy outer surface. The exposed upper tips of the leaves are flattened or convex, with an area of translucent cells called a fenestration or light window. This feature allows light to enter the interior of the leaves that are otherwise shielded from the sun. The plant produces crystalline fibers in its interior that assist the transmission of light deeper into the leaf. Solitary flowers are borne on short stalks between the exposed leaf tips. The flowers can be up to 8 cm in diameter, with numerous white or yellow strap-shaped, petal-like structures derived from staminodes.

ORIGIN AND HABITAT: It is native to South Africa and Namibia, found in the Namib desert, and growing in very sandy soils.

BABY ELEPHANT'S FEET

COMMON NAME(S)
Baby Elephant's Feet,
Fairy Elephant's Feet,
Glasies, Baby Toes,
Purple Baby Tears

SCIENTIFIC NAME
Frithia pulchra

GENUS ETYMOLOGY: In honor of British-born South African horticulturist Frank Frith (1872–1954).

SPECIES ETYMOLOGY: From the Latin word for "beautiful" (*pulcher*).

CORE CHARACTERISTICS: A small, rosette-forming perennial closely related to *Fenestraria rhopalophylla* (pages 30–31). It remains partially to mostly buried, with just the upper portions of the leaves above ground. The grayish-green leaves are up to 2 cm long and 5 mm in diameter, with the tips flattened or convex. The tips have a fenestration, or light window, to allow sunlight to enter the leaf's interior. The leaves are club-shaped, appearing very similar to *F. rhopalophylla*, but are more tubular or cylindrical. The inflorescence is also very similar to *F. rhopalophylla*, producing solitary, daisy-like flowers around 30 mm in diameter that are either stalkless or on a very short stalk. Unlike *F. rhopalophylla*, *Frithia*'s flowers are magenta.

ORIGIN AND HABITAT: It is native to South Africa, inhabiting high-altitude grasslands, primarily in shallow, gravelly soils or cracks on exposed bedrock.

KAROO ROSE

COMMON NAME(S)
Karoo Rose,
Split Rock

SCIENTIFIC NAME
Lapidaria margaretae

GENUS ETYMOLOGY: From the Latin words for "stone" and "relating to" (*lapis* and *aria*).

SPECIES ETYMOLOGY: Honors South African teacher and plant collector Margarethe Friedrich (birth and death dates unknown).

CORE CHARACTERISTICS: A compact, stemless plant bearing two to four pairs of stone-like leaves, with cultivated plants often producing more. The leaves are triangular and keeled in shape, with rounded edges, and are generally 2–3 cm long and wide. They are grayish white and tend to be darker near their base, with occasionally a pinkish blush. Each pair of leaves is perpendicular to the other, with only a minute space between them, thus appearing as if they are stacked together. Solitary flowers on short stalks emerge from the tip of the plant. They are around 5 cm in diameter and daisy-like in appearance, with about 100 bright yellow petals and 300–500 erect stamens.

ORIGIN AND HABITAT: It is known from only about fifteen locations in southern Namibia and the Northern Cape province of South Africa. It inhabits sandy and rocky soils in full sun or under small shrubs. It is often mostly buried and inconspicuous to the naked eye.

LITHOPS

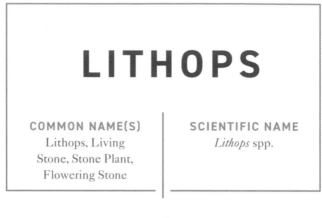

COMMON NAME(S)
Lithops, Living
Stone, Stone Plant,
Flowering Stone

SCIENTIFIC NAME
Lithops spp.

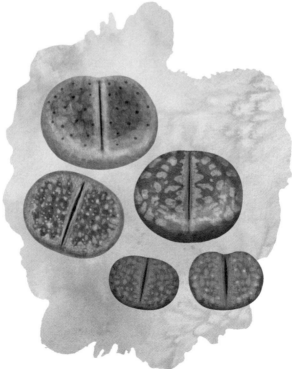

GENUS ETYMOLOGY: From the Greek words for "stone" and "face" (*lithos* and *ops*).

CORE CHARACTERISTICS: A genus of at least thirty-seven species of succulent plants with "uniquely modified" leaves. Individual plants consist of only a taproot with two fleshy, fused leaves that may only partially emerge above the soil surface, rarely exceeding 2.5 cm in height. The leaves are primarily thick and bulbous, with a flattened exposed surface. Each leaf is up to 3 cm in diameter, depending on the species. The coloration is variable among the species but tends to be earth-toned, such as gray, brown, and green, to best blend in with their substrate. The exposed leaf surfaces have fenestrations, allowing more light to reach the plant. These fenestrations are variously colored, usually darker than the leaf, and form various patterns and colors. Exposed leaf surfaces may also be somewhat textured, usually with dimples. These characteristics help the plant survive extremely arid habitats and result in a plant that resembles a small stone on the ground, blending in with its environment. The camouflage is so effective that it is often difficult for even skilled naturalists to detect them in their natural habitats. Small, daisy-like flowers emerge from between the leaves primarily during the fall or winter.

ORIGIN AND HABITAT: They are native to southern Africa, in numerous widely-scattered populations in sandy or rocky habitats.

BUNNY SUCCULENT

COMMON NAME(S)
Bunny Succulent,
String of Beads/
Pearls, Beaded Vygie,
Beaded Ice Plant

SCIENTIFIC NAME
Monilaria spp.

GENUS ETYMOLOGY: From the Latin words for "necklace" and "connected with" (*monile* and *aria*).

CORE CHARACTERISTICS: A genus of about sixteen heterophyllic species with succulent leaves and stems. These plants are characterized by producing two different kinds of leaves. At the start of each rainy season, a new, bead-shaped leaf is produced at the tip of the stem, followed by a pair of more conventional cylindrical leaves that are united at the base. The traditional leaves fall off at the end of the rainy season, with the fused leaf base persisting as a bead-shaped sheath. This results in the stem superficially resembling a string of beads, hence one of the common names. It also makes it easy to estimate the age of the plant, as it will produce one "bead" every year. Flowers are solitary and terminal, on long stalks 50–70 mm long. They are usually around 30 mm in diameter, with numerous white to yellowish petals, but other colors, such as orange and red, are occasionally seen.

ORIGIN AND HABITAT: They are native to South Africa, where they can be found in dry, rocky areas, primarily quartzite,

CLOCK PLANT

COMMON NAME(S)
Clock Plant, Rabies,
Banded Nananthus

SCIENTIFIC NAME
Nananthus vittatus
(syn. *Rabiea albipuncta*)

GENUS ETYMOLOGY: From the Greek words for "dwarf" and "flower" (*nános* and *ánthos*).

SPECIES ETYMOLOGY: From the Latin word for "banded" (*vittatus*).

CORE CHARACTERISTICS: A mat-forming plant consisting of dense clumps of rosettes of fleshy leaves. Each rosette has six to eight pairs of leaves up to 30 mm long and 9 mm wide. The leaves are lanceolate in shape with a prominent keel on the lower surface. They are primarily dark or olive green in color, with numerous whitish idioblasts—wart-like projections comprised of specialized storage cells—that impart a rough texture to the leaves. The roots are tuberous and carrot-like, extending up to 20 cm downward. Plants eventually develop a large caudex resembling a tree's trunk, making this a popular bonsai species. Flowers are solitary, emerging from the center of the rosette on a short, thick stalk that barely exceeds the height of the leaves. They are daisy-like and up to 2.5 cm in diameter, with numerous yellow petals that occasionally have a reddish blush at their tips.

ORIGIN AND HABITAT: It is native to northern portions of South Africa, where it occurs in dense, grassy areas and often in soils that are loamier than those other succulents tend to be found in.

CORAL PLANT

COMMON NAME(S)
Coral Plant

SCIENTIFIC NAME
Neohenricia sibbettii

GENUS ETYMOLOGY: From the Ancient Greek word for "new." (*neos*) and in honor of Swiss-born South African scientist Marguerite Gertrud Anna Henrici (1892–1971).

SPECIES ETYMOLOGY: Unresolved.

CORE CHARACTERISTICS: A tiny, creeping perennial that forms mats up to 30 cm in diameter and 1 cm high. It has ascending to erect club-shaped leaves that are borne in pairs and fused at their bases. They can grow up to 10 mm long and 4 mm wide, have a brownish to a greenish color, and are covered by wart-like protuberances, primarily near the apex. The small size, along with the physical appearance, makes specimens easily blend into their surroundings. Flowers are solitary and star-shaped, around 15 mm in diameter, with white to pale green petals that may have purplish tips. Despite their small size, the flowers emit a powerful fruity fragrance that can be detected several meters away

ORIGIN AND HABITAT: It is native to South Africa, with several disjointed populations occurring throughout. It is mainly found in the crevices of rocks, primarily sandstone.

DEW PLANT

COMMON NAME(S)
Dew Plant, Pink
Ice Plant, Deltoid-
Leaved Dew Plant

SCIENTIFIC NAME
Oscularia deltoides

GENUS ETYMOLOGY: From the Latin words for "mouth" and "possessing" (*osculum* and *aria*).

SPECIES ETYMOLOGY: From the Ancient Greek word for "triangular" (*deltoeidis*).

CORE CHARACTERISTICS: A compact but sprawling perennial with a height of around 30 cm and an indefinite width. It produces shiny, purplish-tinged stems that branch freely and are densely packed together. The leaves are thick and fleshy, with a deltoid to a triangular shape and bluntly-toothed margins. They are bluish green in color and pruinose, up to 18 mm long and 10 mm wide. The daisy-like flowers are borne in cymes, with up to three flowers in a cluster. They are around 3 cm in diameter, with numerous pink to purple petals surrounding a yellow center.

ORIGIN AND HABITAT. It is native to the South West Cape of South Africa, where it remains shaded for most of the day in the crevices of steep sandstone rocks. It also has been naturalized in England on coastal rocks and walls on the Isles of Scilly.

CONCRETE LEAF

COMMON NAME(S)
Concrete Leaf,
Jewel Plant, Sheep's
Tongue, Carpet Leaf

SCIENTIFIC NAME
Titanopsis calcarea

GENUS ETYMOLOGY: Unresolved, may refer to the Titans of Greek mythology or an Ancient Greek word for limestone (*titanos*).

SPECIES ETYMOLOGY: From the Latin word for "of lime" (*calcarius*).

CORE CHARACTERISTICS: A perennial up to 10 cm in diameter and 3 cm in height, forming mats of closely packed rosettes over time. Leaves are fleshy and broadly ovate or tongue-shaped, up to 2.5 cm long and 1.5 cm wide, often wrinkly, and typically grayish to blue-green. The upper portions of the leaves are densely covered by variously sized round and flat tubercules that may be whitish, brownish, reddish, or bluish. They impart a pebbly appearance to the leaves, which acts as camouflage. Solitary, daisy-like flowers emerge from the base of the rosette. They are up to 2 cm in diameter, with numerous yellow to orange petals.

ORIGIN AND HABITAT: It is native to the Bushmanland and Upper Karoo regions of South Africa, where it grows primarily on limestone outcrops

ANACAMPSEROTACEAE

Avonia

A small family of three genera and thirty-six species that are primarily found in southern and eastern Africa, along with a small number of species in Australia, North America, and South America. This is a relatively new family, named and described in 2010 due to molecular and morphological analyses. The species in this family were formerly part of the Purslane family (Portulacaceae). They are all leaf succulents and are considered either herbaceous perennials or subshrubs.

AVONIA USTULATA

COMMON NAME(S)

Avonia ustulata,
Kirriemoer,
Moerbossie

SCIENTIFIC NAME

Avonia ustulata

GENUS ETYMOLOGY: Unresolved.

SPECIES ETYMOLOGY: From the Latin word for "scorched."

CORE CHARACTERISTICS: A tiny, slow-growing shrub that attains a height of only about 8 cm. From a partially buried caudex, it produces numerous dichotomously dividing, wormlike branches. The branches reach up to 2.5 cm in length and 2 mm in diameter. They are silvery gray in color and covered by densely overlapping papery scales. The true leaves are minuscule and covered by these scales. The result is a plant resembling a tangled mass of worms or caterpillars. It is believed that the plant's form evolved as a bird-dropping mimic as a form of camouflage. Tiny, cream-colored flowers are produced at the tips of fertile branches and open only during the afternoon on hot days.

ORIGIN AND HABITAT: It is native to South Africa and tends to grow directly on exposed shales.

APOCYNACEAE

Ceropegia   *Larryleachia*   *Tavaresia*

Dischidia   *Orbea*   *Tromotriche*

Huernia   *Pseudolithos*

A large family of at least 366 genera and around 5,100 species. It is mainly known as the Dogbane or Milkweed family. It has a global distribution, with most species found in tropical and subtropical regions. A variety of growth forms can be found in the family, including herbaceous annuals and perennials, shrubs, vines, trees, and stem succulents. They all have simple leaves, primarily opposite or whorled in arrangement. The flowers are generally five-parted, radially symmetrical, and with the petals at least partially fused into a tubular shape. Many species contain milky latex or are poisonous. Pollen is transported as a mass of pollen grains called a pollinium.

STRING OF HEARTS

COMMON NAME(S)
String of Hearts,
Rosary Vine,
Sweetheart Vine

SCIENTIFIC NAME
Ceropegia woodii

GENUS ETYMOLOGY: From the Ancient Greek word for "candlestick" (*keropegion*).

SPECIES ETYMOLOGY: Honors South African botanist John Medley Wood (1827–1915).

CORE CHARACTERISTICS: A trailing evergreen plant that reaches 10 cm in height. The stems are thin and woody, spreading up to 4 m long. The fleshy, heart-shaped leaves are arranged in opposite pairs along the stems, up to 2 cm wide and long. The leaves are dark green with a silvery sheen when growing in sunlight. They are much paler if growing in a shady area. Tubers can form on roots and stems (aerial tubers). Flowers appear during the summer and are tubular, with five petals fused at their very tips, creating a cage-like structure over the flower's opening. They are usually around 3–4 cm long, with a color ranging from pale pink to purple.

ORIGIN AND HABITAT: It is native to southern Africa, from Zimbabwe to South Africa, where it is primarily found on rocky outcrops and ledges in forested habitats

ANT PLANT

COMMON NAME(S)
Ant Plant, Kangaroo
Plant, Bladder Vine

SCIENTIFIC NAME
Dischidia vidalii (syn.
Dischidia pectinoides)

GENUS ETYMOLOGY: From the Greek words for "twice" and "to separate" (*di-* and *schizo*).

SPECIES ETYMOLOGY: In honor of Spanish botanist Sebastián Vidal y Soler (1842–1889).

CORE CHARACTERISTICS: A myrmecophilous, perennial, epiphytic vine that reaches lengths of up to 3 m. The stems are thin and contain a milky sap. The fleshy leaves are opposite in arrangement, ovate to elliptical, up to 3 cm long and 1.5 cm wide, and pale green. Some modified leaves, called ascidia, occur intermittently along the stem. These leaves are bladder-like with a single small (2 mm) opening. They can grow up to 7 cm long and 5 cm wide, with the outer surface the same color as the typical leaves. The inner surface is a brownish red, and additional roots grow inside. These ascidia attract and host ant colonies that provide a nutrient source to the plant through their excrement and other organic substances absorbed by the roots inside. Inflorescences are borne in axillary clusters of usually three to six flowers. The flowers are urceolate in shape and up to 1 cm long. They have five petals fused along almost their entire length and are red to magenta.

ORIGIN AND HABITAT: It is native to the Philippines, primarily growing on bamboo plants at low elevations.

LIFESAVER PLANT

COMMON NAME(S)
Lifesaver Plant

SCIENTIFIC NAME
Huernia spp.

GENUS ETYMOLOGY: In honor of Dutch physician and avid plant collector Justus Huernius (1587–1652).

CORE CHARACTERISTICS: A genus of about seventy-seven species of perennial stem succulents. Small, clump-forming plants produce procumbent to erect fleshy four- to five-angled stems, rarely over 10 cm in height. They are usually some shade of green but may be more olive or yellowish in some species. The angles are covered by tubercules, from which rudimentary leaves may emerge. In some species these rudimentary leaves look like spines; in others, they are barely visible. The inflorescence is a cyme that originates from the base of the stems. Individual flowers are five parted and funnel- or bell-shaped, typically 2–3 cm in width. They range in color from yellow to brown to red and are often intricately patterned or striped in contrasting colors and may be glossy and wrinkled in appearance. The flowers are pollinated by flies, which are attracted to the carrion-like odor and appearance of the flowers.

ORIGIN AND HABITAT: They are native to the Arabian Peninsula and southern and eastern Africa, with the typical habitat being dry, rocky, and scrubby.

LARRYLEACHIA

COMMON NAME(S)
Larryleachia, Cactus
Barrel Milkweed

SCIENTIFIC NAME
Larryleachia cactiformis
(syn. Trichocaulon
cactiforme)

GENUS ETYMOLOGY: In honor of Leslie Charles "Larry" Leach (1909–1996), an English-born South African electrical engineer and botany enthusiast.

SPECIES ETYMOLOGY: From the word cactus and the Latin word for "having the form of" (*-formis*).

CORE CHARACTERISTICS: A small, perennial stem succulent, up to 30 cm tall and 60 mm wide, with a cactus-like appearance. The stems are usually unbranched and globular or cylindrical, with a green to blue-green color. The surface is tessellated by irregular five-sided flat or slightly concave tubercules. The leaves are reduced to tiny appressed scales up to 1 mm long. Flowers are produced in clusters of one to five from tubercules at the tip of the stem, on 1 mm peduncles, making the flowers appear stalkless. Each flower is up to 10 mm in diameter and tubular, with five triangular lobes. The base flower color is cream to pale pink, with dark reddish markings. The interior surface is bristly and papillate. The flowers have a specialized pollination mechanism that involves attracting and partially trapping flies, resulting in the attachment of pollinia to their bodies. When the flies finally escape, the pollinia remain attached and are carried with them to the next flower they visit.

ORIGIN AND HABITAT: It is native to Namibia and South Africa, where it is a common inhabitant of rocky flatlands and slopes.

STARFISH PLANT

COMMON NAME(S)
Starfish Plant, Toad
Plant, Carrion Plant

SCIENTIFIC NAME
Orbea variegata

GENUS ETYMOLOGY: From the Latin word for "ring" (*orbis*).

SPECIES ETYMOLOGY: From the Latin word for "variegated" (*varius*).

CORE CHARACTERISTICS: A soft-stemmed and sprawling perennial, attaining heights of approximately 10 cm and spreading to 50 cm. The four-angled glabrous stems branch and form large clumps over time. Depending on sun exposure, they are grayish green with various amounts of purple mottling. It is a leafless plant with stems adorned with teeth-like tubercules along the angles. It bears large flowers, up to 8 cm in diameter, with five blunt lobes. Flowers emit a carrion-like odor. They are greenish yellow in color but are heavily marked with reddish-brown blotches. The flowers vaguely resemble a starfish, hence one of the common names. Seed pods are narrow and cylindrical, up to 12 cm long, and contain numerous seeds with a tuft of white hairs. When ripe, the seed pods burst open and release the seeds to be dispersed by the wind.

ORIGIN AND HABITAT: It is native to the Eastern Cape province of South Africa, where it is generally found on rocky slopes, primarily right on exposed rock surfaces, but occasionally in the shade of larger shrubs.

PSEUDOLITHOS

COMMON NAME(S)
Pseudolithos,
False Stone

SCIENTIFIC NAME
Pseudolithos spp.

GENUS ETYMOLOGY: From the Greek word for "false" (*psevdís*) and the Latin word for "stone" (*lithos*).

CORE CHARACTERISTICS: A small genus containing ten species of leafless, pebble-mimicking stem succulents. They are characterized by having small, clump-forming stems typically no more than 10 cm tall or wide. The shape of the stems can be globular, cylindrical, or nearly amorphous, depending on the species. They are usually grayish green or pale brown and covered by variously sized and shaped tubercules, with some species resembling the skin of a crocodile or snake. Inflorescences are borne in clusters of four to thirty flowers that emerge in scattered locations across the stems. Individual flowers are five-parted and star-shaped, usually around 5 mm in diameter. The flower color ranges from grayish green to maroon, and they emit a carrion-like odor to attract pollinating flies.

ORIGIN AND HABITAT: All species are native to dry environments in Oman, Somalia, and Yemen, inhabiting open areas with gritty soils.

DEVIL'S TRUMPET

COMMON NAME(S)
Devil's Trumpet,
Thimble Flower,
Tavaresia

SCIENTIFIC NAME
Tavaresia barklyi

GENUS ETYMOLOGY: In honor of Portuguese naturalist Joaquim da Silva Tavares (1866–1931).

SPECIES ETYMOLOGY: In honor of the British colonial administrator in South Africa, Sir Henry Barkly (1815–1898).

CORE CHARACTERISTICS: A multi-stemmed, densely tufted, and cactus-like perennial, reaching up to 6 cm in height and 12 cm in diameter. Each stem is cylindrical, erect, and up to 1.5 cm in diameter. They are glabrous and bluish green, often with a purplish blush that can become quite dark under intense sunlight. The stems have five to fourteen vertically oriented ribs with closely-set tubercules along the apex. Each tubercule has three sharp spines or bristles around 0.5 cm long. One of the spines is aligned perpendicular to the stem, while the other two are more or less parallel. Showy flowers emerge from the base of the stems in clusters of one to four, opening successively. They are relatively large and trumpet-shaped, up to 11 cm long and 2.5 cm in diameter. The flower color ranges from cream to yellowish. It is heavily dappled with maroon speckles and streaks and becomes solidly maroon in the interior base of the flower. The fruit is a large, elongated follicle containing numerous seeds with tufts of hair to facilitate wind dispersal.

ORIGIN AND HABITAT: It is native to a broad swath of southern Africa, growing on rocky outcrops and sandy plains.

REVOLUTE-FLOWERED TROMOTRICHE

COMMON NAME(S)
Revolute-Flowered
Tromotriche

SCIENTIFIC NAME
Tromotriche revoluta
(syn. *Stapelia revoluta*)

GENUS ETYMOLOGY: From the Greek word for "trembling" (*trómos*) and the Latin word for "hairs" (*trichos*).

SPECIES ETYMOLOGY: From the Latin word for "rolled back" (*revolvo*).

CORE CHARACTERISTICS: A rhizomatous, sparingly branched stem–succulent shrub up to 45 cm tall. The erect stems are 15–45 cm high and 1.5–3 cm in diameter, glabrous, with a glaucous green color. They are more or less square in cross section (four-angled), with small 2–3 mm long teeth along the apex of each angle. The stems appear leafless, although the leaves are reduced to tiny, barely visible greenish to purplish conical structures. Flowers are borne in clusters of one to three along the upper parts of the stem on short (6–15 mm) pedicels. They are up to 5 cm in diameter, with five recurved lobes that often touch the back of the flower. The outer surface of the flower is yellowish green, while the inner surface is a pale violet to purple brown, with paler worm-like markings. The lobe margins have long, club-shaped purple hairs that vibrate with the slightest breeze.

ORIGIN AND HABITAT: It is native to the Western and Northern Capes of South Africa and commonly found in dry habitats, typically in the shade of larger shrubs.

ASPARAGACEAE

Agave   *Mangave*

A large monocot family of 114 genera and about 2,900 species
that were formerly part of the Lily family (Liliaceae). It includes
many well known plants including asparagus, hosta, yucca,
and hyacinth. The family is morphologically diverse, but most
are herbaceous or shrubby perennials with small rhizomes and
fleshy tubers. Flowers are six-parted and generally tubular and
resemble lily flowers. The fruits are often red or blue berries
with black seeds.

AGAVE

COMMON NAME(S)
Agave, Century Plant

SCIENTIFIC NAME
Agave spp.

GENUS ETYMOLOGY: From the Greek word for "noble, illustrious" (*agauós*).

CORE CHARACTERISTICS: A large genus of approximately 250 species (and numerous hybrids and horticultural varieties) of mostly monocarpic perennials. They are characterized by their rosettes of thick leaves that originate from a short stem, giving the appearance of being stemless. The leaves range in size from a few centimeters to 3 m in length, depending on the species. They may be extended, thin, short, broad, straight, curved, or occasionally irregularly twisted. Most species have leaves with toothed or spiny margins, often with a stiff spine at the tip of the leaf as well. Leaf colors range from bluish gray to green and may have stripes or striations, often strikingly. Inflorescences are borne on stalks that emerge from the center of the rosette. In some species, these stalks may reach 12 m in height. Flowers are six-parted, tubular, and mostly greenish, yellow, or red. While most species are insect-pollinated, some are pollinated by bats or birds. In the monocarpic species, the rosette dies after the seeds ripen. However, many species asexually reproduce before flowering through clonal offsets from the base of the stem or rhizomes or via the production of bulbils on the flowering stems. Additionally, many species may live for decades before producing a flowering stem. Humans have used Agave for many purposes, including as a source of fiber, a sweetener, a food source, a medicine, an ornamental , and in the production of certain liquors.

ORIGIN AND HABITAT: They are native to the Americas, reaching as far north as the state of Utah and as far south as northern South America, with some species also found on Caribbean islands. Mexico has the greatest diversity of species. Most species are found in semi-arid habitats at elevations higher than true deserts. Typical habitats include dry grasslands and dry oak-pine woodlands.

MANGAVE

COMMON NAME(S)
Mangave,
Macho Mocha

SCIENTIFIC NAME
Mangave spp.

GENUS ETYMOLOGY: A combination of *Manfreda* and *Agave*.

CORE CHARACTERISTICS: *Mangave* were formerly considered intergeneric hybrids between *Manfreda* and *Agave* species, initially discovered among wild-collected seed from northern Mexico and later artificially produced by plant breeders. However, recent studies have shown that *Manfreda* spp. should be included in *Agave*, rendering the genus *Manfreda* and the hybrid name x *Mangave* obsolete. However, because numerous cultivars were bred and put on the market under the name "Mangave," the name continues to be used in horticultural circles. As a group, *Mangave* cultivars are somewhat distinct from other *Agave* species. They tend to be more vigorous, produce fewer offshoots than other *Agave*, and are more tolerant of wetter and shadier conditions than *Agave* typically grow in. Leaf colors can be green, blue, red, or purple, and are often two-toned with variously shaped markings. The leaves also lack teeth commonly found on other *Agave* species. Inflorescences are borne on a tall stalk (up to 2 m), with the flowers ranging from yellowish to golden brown.

ORIGIN AND HABITAT: Not applicable—this is a human-created hybrid.

ASPHODELACEAE

Astrolista   *Haworthia*   *Trachyandra*

Gasteria

A family of 40 genera and about 900 species of monocots referred to as the Aloe family that was formerly part of the Lily family. It includes a variety of growth forms, including herbaceous annuals and perennials, shrubs, trees, and vines. It is a morphologically diverse family with few characteristics common to all species. Most are rhizomatous with linear or lanceolate leaves that form a basal rosette or a terminal cluster. Flowers are mostly borne in spikes or racemes on a leafless stalk and consist of six tepals that are either star-shaped or fused into a tube.

ASTROLISTA

COMMON NAME(S)
Astrolista,
Astroworthia

SCIENTIFIC NAME
Astrolista bicarinata
(syn. *Astroworthia
bicarinata*)

GENUS ETYMOLOGY: A portmanteau of the parental genera.

SPECIES ETYMOLOGY: The Latin word for "two-keeled."

CORE CHARACTERISTICS: A subshrub that is a naturally occurring intergeneric hybrid between *Astroloba corrugata* and *Tulista pumila*. Because it is a hybrid, there is some variability in the appearance of each individual. However, they all display hybrid vigor: they are more prominent in almost all aspects, compared to both parental species, reaching heights of up to 1 m. The leaves are fleshy, triangular, and keeled, often with two keels. They can grow up to 10 cm long and 3 cm wide on mature individuals. Their color starts green, slowly turning reddish over time. The leaves are covered by numerous small, white tubercules, making the leaves superficially resemble starfish legs. Small white six-parted flowers are produced on tall, branching racemes.

ORIGIN AND HABITAT: They are found only where the range of the two parental species overlap, which is in the Little Karoo region of South Africa. There they occur in dry, rocky habitats.

OX TONGUE

COMMON NAME(S)
Ox Tongue, Cow
Tongue, Lawyer's
Tongue

SCIENTIFIC NAME
Gasteria spp.

GENUS ETYMOLOGY: From the Greek word for "belly" (*gaster*).

CORE CHARACTERISTICS: A genus of shade-tolerant plants that remains taxonomically unresolved regarding the number of species. Molecular studies seem to put the number around thirty-eight, but there is still disagreement within the scientific community. They are characterized by flattened triangular or tongue-shaped leaves in a distichous arrangement, meaning they are produced alternately in two opposite rows along the stem. The leaves range in length from 3 to 30 cm, depending on the species. Older plants may appear more rosette-like. The leaves are fleshy yet brittle, have a waxy coating, and are variously adorned with spots, bands, or warty tubercules. The inflorescences are produced on a long-stalked raceme that may reach 1 m in height. Individual flowers are pendant and tubular, with a distinct bulbous base, hence the generic name. Flower colors range from orange to pink to red, often with paler tips.

ORIGIN AND HABITAT: Most species are native to the Eastern Cape of South Africa. One species is found in Namibia, and another in Eswatini. They tend to inhabit rocky habitats, growing in the shade of larger shrubs.

HAWORTHIA

COMMON NAME(S)
Haworthia, Pearl
Plant, Star Window
Plant, Zebra Cactus

SCIENTIFIC NAME
Haworthia spp.

GENUS ETYMOLOGY: In honor of English botanist Adrian Hardy Haworth (1767–1883).

CORE CHARACTERISTICS: A genus of approximately 150 species of small succulents, similar to aloe's overall form. They form rosettes of thick fleshy leaves, mostly less than 3 cm in diameter, with a few species reaching up to 30 cm in diameter. Most species are stemless and form basal rosettes, but some species grow up to 0.5 m in height. The leaves are highly variable between the various species, with an array of leaf thickness and texture, coloration, and leaf markings (or lack thereof) present. Many species have fenestrations, or light windows, on the upper surface of their leaves. Some species grow as solitary individuals, while others can form large clumps over time. The flowers are small, white, tubular, and borne on spikes that can reach up to 0.5 m in height, depending on the species.

ORIGIN AND HABITAT: They are native to southern Africa, primarily in the Cape of South Africa, where they can be found in various semi-arid habitats such as savannas, thickets, and heathlands, at a variety of altitudes, and in sandy, rocky soils.

RIBBON PLANT

COMMON NAME(S)
Ribbon Plant

SCIENTIFIC NAME
Trachyandra tortilis

GENUS ETYMOLOGY: From the Greek words for "rough" and "man" (*trachýs* and *ándras*).

SPECIES ETYMOLOGY: From the Latin word for "twisted" (*torquere*).

CORE CHARACTERISTICS: A stemless, perennial geophyte that grows up to 25 cm tall. It consists of a large, scaly, underground tuber from which three to six widely spreading basal leaves emerge. Each ribbon-like leaf is 10 cm long and 2 cm wide, linear in shape, and flat in cross section, primarily glabrous but occasionally with sparse pubescence. Each leaf is uniquely transversely and plicately folded and coiled, resulting in a sinuous appearance when viewed laterally. Inflorescences are borne in ascending but lax panicles up to 10 cm long. They have up to 5 divaricate side branches, each with a few to several flowers. Each flower is radially symmetrical and star-shaped, about 2 cm in diameter, with six white to pale pink tepals.

ORIGIN AND HABITAT: It is native to the Northern and Western Cape provinces of South Africa, growing in sandy soils, in dry riverbeds, and on quartzite outcrops.

ASTERACEAE

Senecio

One of the largest plant families and perhaps one of the most easily recognized. It contains at least 1,900 genera and over 32,000 species and can be found everywhere except Antarctica. Most members are herbaceous annuals, biennials, or perennials, but some representatives are shrubs, vines, and trees. There are a variety of shapes and sizes and a few unifying characteristics among all species. Most species have a large taproot and have lobed or incised leaves. The one characteristic they all share is their unique type of composite flower. A composite flower consists of a densely packed cluster of tiny flowers called a capitulum. The capitulum consists of up to two kinds of flowers: disc flowers and ray flowers. Many species have both, but some have only one or the other. Disc flowers are radially symmetrical, consisting of fused petals forming a five-lobed tubular flower. Ray flowers consist of two- or three-lobed, strap-shaped petals formed by fused petals. When both flower types are present, you end up with your stereotypical daisy-like flower: the petals are a ring of ray flowers surrounding the central cluster of disc flowers.

BLUE CHALK STICKS

COMMON NAME(S)
Blue Chalk Sticks,
Bluefinger, Blue
Straws, Narrow Leaf
Chalk-Sticks

SCIENTIFIC NAME
*Senecio talinoides (*syn.
*Curio talinoides, Senecio
mandraliscae)*

GENUS ETYMOLOGY: From the Latin word for "old man" (*senex*).

SPECIES ETYMOLOGY: A combination of the genus *Talinum* and the Latin word for "resembles" (*oides*).

CORE CHARACTERISTICS: An erect evergreen shrub that often becomes procumbent over time, with sprawling stems that root at the nodes. It reaches a height of around 40 cm, and older individuals can sprawl to at least 60 cm wide. The leaves are produced in clusters at the tip of the stems and are primarily fusiform or terete in shape, erect or arching, up to 15 cm long and 15 mm in diameter. They are bluish green but are usually covered by a thick pruina that imparts a glaucous gray appearance. The inflorescence is a corymb that can reach up to 40 cm in height and bears up to one hundred composite flowers. The flowers lack ray flowers, thus appearing to lack petals, and are comprised of whitish disc flowers.

ORIGIN AND HABITAT: It is native to the Karoo of South Africa and is primarily found on steep, rocky slopes and cliffs.

CACTACEAE

Cleistocactus   *Opuntia*   *Rhipsalis*

Mammillaria

A very well-known family of 127 genera and approximately
1,750 species of primarily spiny stem succulents. All but one
species are strictly native to the Americas, and that one species
is thought to have been brought to the Old World via birds. In
most species, the leaves are reduced to spines, and the stems are
specialized to store water. The spines grow from modified and
reduced shoots called areoles. The areoles tend to look like small
tufts of hair or fuzz. Flowers also emerge from areoles and are
generally large, tubular, and often showy. Cacti exhibit many
growth forms and may be tree-like, consist of cylindrical or
flattened stems that may be branching, or small and pincushion-
like. It is believed that cacti evolved from traditional shrubs or
trees that may have been partially succulent. Because they are
native to the Americas only, they likely didn't appear until after
the continents drifted apart 100–150 million years ago. Recent
molecular studies indicate that they first appeared 30–35 million
years ago.

GOLDEN RAT TAIL CACTUS

COMMON NAME(S)
Golden Rat Tail
Cactus, Monkey
Tail Cactus

SCIENTIFIC NAME
Cleistocactus winteri
(syn. *Hildewintera*
colademononis)

GENUS ETYMOLOGY: From the Greek words for "closed" and "cactus" (*kleistos* and *káktos*).

SPECIES ETYMOLOGY: Unresolved, perhaps in honor of Hildegarda Winter (1893–1975), the sister of a German nursery owner.

CORE CHARACTERISTICS: A species of columnar cactus with cylindrical, many-branched stems that are arching, drooping, or trailing, forming a tangled mass over time. The stems can reach 1.5 m in length and 6 cm in width. They are densely covered with brown arcoles, each producing a cluster of approximately fifty spines, thus completely covering the stem surface. The spines are straight but flexible, ranging in length from 5–10 mm, and may be white, golden yellow, or golden brown. Flowers are solitary, emerging intermittently along the stems. They are funnel-shaped, up to 5 cm in width and length, with numerous orange to pink tepals. The outer tepals are recurved, while the inner tepals are erect. Fruits are barrel-shaped, approximately 10 mm long and wide, and green or greenish red in color.

ORIGIN AND HABITAT: It is native to the province of Florida in Bolivia, where it is known from only two isolated locations within an area of approximately 250 square kilometers. They grow on forested cliffs in Andes mountain valleys.

PINCUSHION CACTUS

COMMON NAME(S)
Pincushion Cactus,
Globe Cactus,
Birthday Cake
Cactus, Nipple
Cactus

SCIENTIFIC NAME
Mammillaria spp.

GENUS ETYMOLOGY: From the Latin word for "nipple" (*mammilla*).

CORE CHARACTERISTICS: One of the largest genera of cacti, with over 200 species and cultivars. *Mammillaria* species are distinguished from other cacti by having cleft areolae, the small globular structures from which the spines emerge. Most species tend to be small, globular, and covered with variously shaped tubercules arranged in a spiral pattern, with many species having hooked spines. Species are either single-stemmed or form clumps of stems. Most species are no more than 40 cm tall and 20 cm wide. The flowers range up to 7 cm in diameter and form in a ring around the upper surface of the plant. They are comprised of numerous lanceolate tepals that may be white, yellow, pink, or red. The fruit is berry-like, juicy, somewhat cylindrical, and may be white, green, pink, or red.

ORIGIN AND HABITAT: They are native from Central America to the southern United States, with the most significant number and diversity of species occurring in Mexico. They are present in a variety of environments, including hot and cold deserts, conifer forests, and moist tropical forests.

PRICKLY PEAR CACTUS

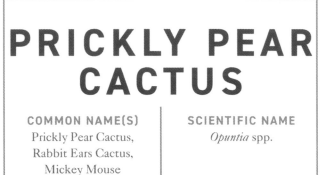

COMMON NAME(S)
Prickly Pear Cactus,
Rabbit Ears Cactus,
Mickey Mouse
Cactus

SCIENTIFIC NAME
Opuntia spp.

GENUS ETYMOLOGY: Named after the ancient Greek city of Opus.

CORE CHARACTERISTICS: A large genus of cacti containing over 150 species and numerous hybrids and cultivars. Most species are low-growing and shrub-like, although some tree-like species approach 5 m in height. They are characterized by flattened, jointed, and branching cladodes that are usually paddle-shaped or cylindrical. The cladodes are adorned with areoles that produce spines and short, bristle-like structures called glochidia. The spines vary in length and orientation and may be absent in some species. The glochidia have a hooked tip, making them difficult to remove from skin and clothing, and are arguably more of an annoyance than the spines. Flowers are solitary, emerging from the tips of the outermost cladodes. They tend to be large and showy, with numerous tepals ranging from yellow to orange to pink, sometimes with darker markings. Fruits are somewhat variable across the genus, but are generally cylindrical to ovoid in shape. They may be smooth or covered by tubercules or spines, and may be fleshy or dry. Dry fruits are usually some shade of brown, while fleshy fruits are green, yellow, red, or purple. The cladodes and the fleshy fruits are used as a food source by humans and other animals.

ORIGIN AND HABITAT: The various species are widespread in the New World, from Canada to South America, including the West Indies and the Galapagos Islands. Some species have been introduced outside their native range, including Africa, Australia, and the Mediterranean, where they have become invasive. They can be found in various dry habitats, such as sandy soils and exposed bedrock.

MISTLETOE CACTUS

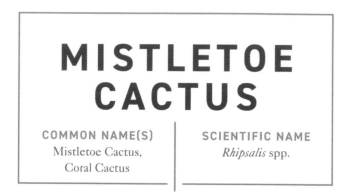

COMMON NAME(S)
Mistletoe Cactus,
Coral Cactus

SCIENTIFIC NAME
Rhipsalis spp.

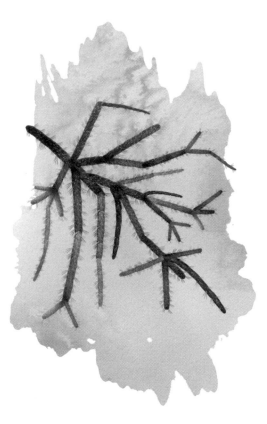

GENUS ETYMOLOGY: From the Ancient Greek word for "wickerwork" (*Rhips*), and the Latin suffix meaning "pertaining to" (*-alis*).

CORE CHARACTERISTICS: A genus of about forty-five species of primarily epiphytic cacti. A few species are lithophytic (growing in rocks). While the morphology of the various species is somewhat variable, most species have cylindrical (terete) stems, with the remaining species having flattened or four-angled stems. The epiphytic species primarily have a pendent growth form, with the stems hanging from the trees they are growing on. A few species have either an upright or sprawling growth form. Unlike most other cacti, nearly every species lacks spines, only has spines during their immature stages, or has very fine, hairlike spines. The flowers are solitary, borne either at the tips of the stems or laterally along their sides. They are among the smallest Cactus family flowers, rarely exceeding 1 cm in diameter. Most species' petals are white, with a few species having red or yellow flowers.

ORIGIN AND HABITAT: They are native to Central America, the Caribbean, and northern South America, as well as parts of Africa and Asia, making this the only group of cacti native to the Old World. Being epiphytic, they are primarily found in forested areas, usually shadier and wetter habitats than other types of cacti. One theory is that migratory birds deposited seeds far enough back in time for the Old World specimens to naturalize, adapt, and be considered native.

COMMELINACEAE

Callisia

A family consisting of forty-one genera and about 730 species, commonly called the Dayflower family or the Spiderwort family. Most species are herbaceous perennials with grass-like alternate leaves that sheath the stem and are often succulent. Also, in most species new leaves emerge with inrolled margins, unfurling as the leaf expands. Flowers are borne in terminal or axillary inflorescences called thyrses. Individual flowers have three petals that may or may not be equal. They lack nectar-producing glands and typically remain open for only a few hours.

ROSELINGS

COMMON NAME(S)
Roselings,
Creeping Inch Plant,
Turtle Vine

SCIENTIFIC NAME
Callisia repens

GENUS ETYMOLOGY: From the Greek word for "beauty" (*kallos*).

SPECIES ETYMOLOGY: From the Latin for "creeping" or "crawling" (*repo*).

CORE CHARACTERISTICS: An herbaceous, creeping, mat-forming perennial that grows up to 30 cm tall and spreads up to 1 m wide. The slender, trailing stems can root at each node and bear alternately arranged glabrous leaves that are broadly ovate to lanceolate. They are up to 4 cm long and 1 cm wide, gradually decreasing in size toward the tip of the stem. Leaf color is typically green but may have white or pink variegations. The underside of the leaf is flushed burgundy. Inflorescences are paired cymes borne in the distal leaf axils of erect flowering stems. The flowers are inconspicuous, with tiny white lanceolate petals.

ORIGIN AND HABITAT: The species is native to the Americas, from Texas and Florida in the United States and the West Indies (Guadeloupe and Martinique) to Argentina. It also has been naturalized in Hong Kong and is considered an invasive species in Australia. It inhabits shady, rocky areas within forested habitats.

CRASSULACEAE

Adromischus	*Kalanchoe*	*Sempervivum*
Crassula	*Monanthes*	*Sinocrassula*
Echeveria	*Pachyveria*	*Umbilicus*
Graptoveria	*Sedum*	

A family of thirty-five genera and about 1,400 species of leaf succulents, usually referred to as the Stonecrop family. Members can be found worldwide but primarily in the Northern Hemisphere and South Africa. They tend to inhabit colder habitats than succulents from other families. All species utilize a type of photosynthesis called Crassulacean acid metabolism (CAM photosynthesis), an adaptation to help conserve moisture within the plant. Most species are herbaceous perennials, with a few shrubs, trees, vines, and epiphytes. They typically have simple leaves with entire or lobed margins, and are flat or round in cross section. Flowers are primarily produced in terminal or axillary thyrses or cymes, with radially-symmetrical five-parted flowers that are mostly white, yellow, or red. Many species are rather cold hardy and have a bizarre appearance, which has led to them being popular indoor and outdoor ornamentals.

PLOVER EGGS PLANT

COMMON NAME(S)
Plover Eggs Plant,
Club-Adromischus

SCIENTIFIC NAME
Adromischus cooperi

GENUS ETYMOLOGY: From the Ancient Greek for "thick stem" (*adros mischos*).

SPECIES ETYMOLOGY: Honors English plant collector Thomas Cooper (1815–1913).

CORE CHARACTERISTICS: This is a small, freely branching perennial, about 10 cm in height and 20 cm in width. It is characterized by its fleshy, tubular leaves which feature a flattened, scalloped tip wider than the rest of the leaf. The leaves are up to 10 cm long and 3 cm wide, pale sea green, and variously mottled with purple-brown spots. Leaf shape ranges from oblong to spatulate, and they are produced in dense whorls that make the plant appear stemless (acaulescent). Flowers are small and tubular, colored white to pink, and borne in racemes on a leafless stalk that can reach 35 cm in height.

ORIGIN AND HABITAT: It is native to the eastern parts of South Africa and is typically found in dry, rocky areas, primarily inhabiting shaded rock crevices.

JADE PLANT

COMMON NAME(S)
Jade Plant,
Friendship Plant

SCIENTIFIC NAME
Crassula ovata

GENUS ETYMOLOGY: From the Latin word for "thick" (*crassus*).

SPECIES ETYMOLOGY: From the Latin word for "egg" (*ovum*).

CORE CHARACTERISTICS: A thick-stemmed, branching evergreen shrub up to 2.5 m in height. Stems are green and succulent when young, becoming brown and woody-appearing in age, although never forming actual woody tissue. Stems bear pairs of opposite, roundish fleshy leaves, mainly near the outer portions of the branch. Leaves can be up to 9 cm long and 4 cm wide. Leaf margins are sharpened and often reddish when growing in sufficient light. Flowers are produced in terminal clusters, bearing several fragrant, star-shaped white to pink-colored flowers, approximately 15 mm in diameter. They are rarely produced under cultivation. It can reproduce asexually via turtles, which readily feed upon the leaves but rarely devour them completely. The uneaten portions left on the ground can root and begin growing new plants.

ORIGIN AND HABITAT: It is native to South Africa and Mozambique and can be found in several different arid habitats, including shrubby forests and rocky slopes and ravines.

HEN AND CHICKS

COMMON NAME(S)
Hen and Chicks

SCIENTIFIC NAME
Echeveria spp.

GENUS ETYMOLOGY: In honor of Mexican artist Atanasio Echeverría y Godoy (1771–1803).

CORE CHARACTERISTICS: A large genus of around 150 species of perennials that form compact, symmetrical rosettes of fleshy leaves. The rosettes can be anywhere from 8–30 cm in diameter, depending on the species. The leaf shapes are generally spatulate or cuneate in shape, with an acuminate tip. Leaf color is quite variable, with grayish green being the most common. Other colors include silvery gray, red, purple, and near black, with some species developing patterned coloration. Leaf textures range from smooth to waxy to fuzzy, with many species having glaucous leaves. Inflorescences are cymes borne on an erect flowering stalk that emerges from the center of the rosette, reaching heights of up to 30 cm. The flowers are five-parted and tubular, with the colors ranging from yellow to pink and all shades in between. The common name of Hen and Chicks refers to the propensity of these plants to form offshoots that are clones of the mother plant. These offshoots eventually break off, at which point natural forces move the offshoot to a different location, where it sets root and begins growing as a separate plant. In addition to the wild species, numerous hybrids and cultivars have been bred, producing an even greater variety of leaf colors and shapes.

Some species of *Echeveria* are native to Mexico and have been used in traditional medicine for their purported healing properties. The plants have been used to treat various ailments including skin conditions, respiratory problems, and digestive issues.

ORIGIN AND HABITAT: They are native to Argentina, Central America, and Mexico, with one species in southern Texas. They generally inhabit rocky outcrops at high elevations.

OPALINA

COMMON NAME(S)	SCIENTIFIC NAME
Opalina, Graptoveria	*Graptoveria* spp.

GENUS ETYMOLOGY: Unresolved.

CORE CHARACTERISTICS: A group of horticulturally created, intergeneric hybrids between various species of *Graptopetalum* and *Echeveria*. Numerous cultivars are available on the market, offering a variety of leaf colors and shapes. They all produce compact rosettes of fleshy leaves, typically cuneate, ovate, or spatulate, often with a pointed tip. They may be waxy or glaucous, with colors ranging from grayish blue or grayish green to green, with many cultivars having a pink, red, or purple blush or being entirely pigmented pink, red, or purple. Flowers are daisy-like, with numerous strap-shaped, petal-like structures derived from staminodes. They range in color from yellow to red and all shades in between.

ORIGIN AND HABITAT: Not applicable—this is a human-made, intergeneric hybrid.

KALANCHOE

COMMON NAME(S)
Kalanchoe, Mother
of Thousands

SCIENTIFIC NAME
Kalanchoe spp.

GENUS ETYMOLOGY: From the Latinized version of the Cantonese word for "temple plant" (*kalanchauhuy*).

CORE CHARACTERISTICS: A genus of approximately 125 species of herbaceous perennials and shrubs and numerous horticultural cultivars and varieties. The largest species can get up to 6 m tall, but most are less than 1 m. The leaves are flatter than most succulent species and usually have toothed or scalloped margins. They may be smooth and waxy or covered with a felt-like bloom. Flowers feature four petals that fuse into a tube and are usually borne in umbellate or cyme-like clusters. The various species display a wide range of flower colors. Some species are also viviparous, forming new plantlets from the leaf edges.

ORIGIN AND HABITAT: They are primarily native to tropical parts of Africa and Madagascar, where they can be found in arid habitats.

MONANTHES

COMMON NAME(S)
Monanthes, Pale
Monanthes

SCIENTIFIC NAME
Monanthes pallens

GENUS ETYMOLOGY: From the Greek words meaning "single" (*mono*) and "flower" (*anthos*).

SPECIES ETYMOLOGY: From the Latin word for "pale" (*palleo*).

CORE CHARACTERISTICS: A tiny, variable perennial species characterized by dense rosettes of around 100 primarily erect leaves that rarely exceed 2 cm in diameter. The leaves are fleshy and spatulate in shape, up to 20 mm long and 5 mm wide, attenuating to a narrower base. They are greenish and have papillose tips. Leaf color generally darkens gradually over time, such that new leaves at the center of the rosette appear a noticeably paler shade of green. Occasionally, glandular hairs are present on the leaves that are otherwise glabrous. Inflorescences are borne on lateral stems that emerge from outer leaf axils, ranging from 3–5 cm in height. Flowers are held individually on 3–10 mm long glandular, hairy pedicels. They are about 4 mm in diameter, with five to seven yellowish petals, and tend to produce a somewhat disagreeable odor.

ORIGIN AND HABITAT: It is native to the Canary Islands, off the northwest coast of Africa, where it is mainly found in the crevices of rocks within dry ravines and canyons.

LITTLE JEWEL

COMMON NAME(S)
Little Jewel

SCIENTIFIC NAME
Pachyveria glauca (syn. Pachyveria haagei)

GENUS ETYMOLOGY: A combination of *Pachyphytum* and *Echeveria*.

SPECIES ETYMOLOGY: From the Greek word for "blue-gray" (*glaukos*).

CORE CHARACTERISTICS: A horticulturally produced, intergeneric hybrid between *Pachyphytum* and *Echeveria*. It forms a dense rosette of thick, slightly curved, cylindrical leaves with pointed tips, ultimately attaining a height and width of approximately 15 cm. The leaves are bluish gray with a dense covering of farina. With sufficient sun exposure, leaf tips become blushed with a purplish color. Inflorescences are borne in many-flowered cymes, with somewhat drooping five-parted flowers with yellowish-orange petals.

ORIGIN AND HABITAT: Not applicable—this species is a human-made, intergeneric hybrid.

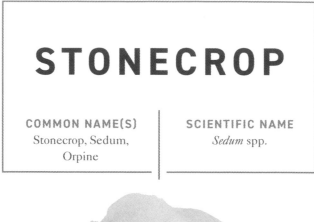

STONECROP

COMMON NAME(S)
Stonecrop, Sedum,
Orpine

SCIENTIFIC NAME
Sedum spp.

GENUS ETYMOLOGY: The Latin word for "houseleek" or "succulent."

CORE CHARACTERISTICS: A large genus of around 500 species of leaf succulents and numerous horticulturally produced hybrids and cultivars exhibiting various morphologies and life forms. Thus, describing the genus itself in great detail is difficult. The various species may be annuals, biennials, or perennials. They range in size and shape from herbaceous, low-growing, mat forming plants to large, semiwoody shrubs. Leaf morphologies range from thick and fleshy down to flattened leaves that do not appear succulent. The leaves may be green to blue to red, or combinations of those colors. Leaf surfaces may be glabrous or glaucous and may or may not have any adornments, such as teeth or tubercles. Inflorescences are axillary or terminal cymes, with radially symmetrical, star-shaped flowers with five to eight petals (mostly five), with twice as many stamens as there are petals. The flower color can be white, yellow, pink, red, or purple. They are very popular ornamental plants, as both houseplants and landscape plants. The primary draw is their overall ease of care, with many cultivars being developed to have attractive leaves and flowers.

ORIGIN AND HABITAT: The genus has a global native distribution, primarily in the Northern Hemisphere, although there are species native south of the equator. Additionally, numerous species have become naturalized or invasive outside their native range, primarily as escapees from cultivation.

LIVE FOREVER

COMMON NAME(S)
Live Forever,
Houseleek,
Hen and Chicks

SCIENTIFIC NAME
Sempervivum spp.

GENUS ETYMOLOGY: From the Latin words for "always" and "living" (*semper* and *vivus*).

CORE CHARACTERISTICS: A genus of about forty species (and numerous horticultural varieties) of rosette-forming, monocarpic perennials with succulent leaves and stems. The leaves range in size from 1.5–6 cm in length, with a lanceolate to ovate shape, often with ciliate margins. In cross section, the leaves range from nearly flat to nearly round. Inflorescence is a terminal cyme borne on a leafy stalk that usually rises three to five times as tall as the rosette. The flowers are radially symmetrical and star-shaped, with eight to sixteen petals that are mostly some shade of pink or purple. Flowers are produced after several years of growth, after which the plant dies. However, numerous clonal offshoots are produced during the years of growth, which become new plants, hence the common names of "Live Forever" and "Hen and Chicks."

ORIGIN AND HABITAT: They are native to Europe and Asia, from the Mediterranean area to Iran, primarily growing in mountainous habitats. They are popular ornamentals due to their ease of care and attractive leaf colors. They are exceptionally cold hardy, surviving down to USDA Zone 4 in the United States.

CHINESE JADE

COMMON NAME(S)
Chinese Jade,
Chocolate Balls,
Hedgehog

SCIENTIFIC NAME
*Sinocrassula
yunnanensis*

GENUS ETYMOLOGY: A combination of the Ancient Greek word for the Chinese (*Sinai*) and the genus *Crassula*.

SPECIES ETYMOLOGY: From the Yunnan province in China, and the Latin word for "from" (*Yunnan* and *ensis*).

CORE CHARACTERISTICS: A small, rosette-forming monocarpic perennial, up to 3.5 cm in diameter and 10 cm in height. Over time, a single plant can develop several rosettes that form a large, dense clump. Each rosette contains fifty to seventy closely packed leaves. The leaves are fleshy, up to 30 mm long and 6 mm wide, ranging from bluish green to olive brown, with tiny purplish-brown speckles and glandular hairs. They are oblanceolate to spatulate in shape, with a mucronate tip. The leaves are loosely attached, often falling off the plant, but they can root and develop into new plants. Inflorescences are borne in a panicle on a leafy stem up to 15 cm in height. Each panicle contains up to fifty tiny, radially-symmetrical, star-shaped flowers. The flowers are up to 1 cm in diameter, with five white petals that may have some pinkish or reddish tinge.

ORIGIN AND HABITAT: It is native to southwest China, northwest India, Sumatra, and Bhutan. It inhabits dry, rocky areas, typically growing from rock crevices.

NAVELWORT

COMMON NAME(S)
Navelwort,
Pennie-Pies, Wall
Pennywort

SCIENTIFIC NAME
Umbilicus rupestris

GENUS ETYMOLOGY: The Latin word for "navel."

SPECIES ETYMOLOGY: From the Latin word for "cliff" (*rupes*).

CORE CHARACTERISTICS: A rosette-forming, perennial geophyte, up to 25 cm in height and 8 cm in diameter. The leaves are fleshy and round, green, and have a scalloped margin. They are depressed centrally on the upper surface (umbilicate), reminiscent of a belly button, hence the common name of "Navelwort." The inflorescence is a terminal raceme on a leafy stem up to 25 cm long, with the leaves progressively decreasing in size from bottom to top. Flowers are tubular, 5–8 mm long, with five ovate petals with a pointed tip. They are yellowish green and hang downward.

ORIGIN AND HABITAT: It is native from Great Britain to North Africa, where it is mainly found growing in damp, shady, rocky areas, including artificial structures such as walls.

CUCURBITACEAE

Xerosicyos

A family of ninety-five genera and about 965 species of primarily herbaceous vines, the rest being lianas, shrubs, or trees. It is mainly called the Gourd family and contains many well-known plants, such as pumpkins, watermelons, and squash. They are native to primarily tropical regions around the world. The stems are usually pentagonal in cross section and variably hairy, with alternate leaves that are palmately lobed or compound and bearing tendrils opposite the leaves. The five-parted flowers are generally tubular and often large, primarily colored white, yellow, or orange. Flowers are unisexual, and plants may be monoecious or dioecious. The fruits are called pepos, modified berries with a thicker outer skin or rind. Cucurbitaceae has one of the highest percentages of species used as human food amongst all plant families.

SILVER DOLLAR PLANT

COMMON NAME(S)
Silver Dollar Plant,
Dollar Vine,
Penny Plant

SCIENTIFIC NAME
Xerosicyos danguyi

GENUS ETYMOLOGY: From the Greek words for "dry" and "cucumber" (*xirós* and *sikuos*).

SPECIES ETYMOLOGY: Honors French botanist Paul A. Danguy (1862–1942).

CORE CHARACTERISTICS: A shrubby vine with slender, branching stems reaching up to 5 m in length. The stems have tiny, forked tendrils that grow opposite each leaf to assist in climbing but will arch over and grow along the ground if there is nothing available to provide support. Simple, fleshy, glabrous leaves are alternately arranged along the stems. They are nearly perfectly round with entire margins and up to 6 cm in diameter. Color ranges from grayish green to blue green. Inflorescences are umbelliform fascicles in the leaf axils that contain up to thirty flowers. The flowers are up to 7 mm in diameter, with four yellowish-green petals. The plants are dioecious.

ORIGIN AND HABITAT: It is native to western and southwestern parts of Madagascar, where it grows in semiarid forests, using various trees to access sunlight in the upper canopy.

PIPERACEAE

Peperomia

A large family of only five genera, but containing around 3,600 species, of which the vast majority are found in only two of those genera. It is commonly called the Pepper family, named after the peppercorn pepper. They have a global distribution, with most species found in tropical or semitropical regions. The family includes herbaceous annuals, perennials, shrubs, and small trees. The leaves are primarily simple and entire and often have a detectable scent when crushed. The inflorescences are borne in mostly terminal or axillary spikes. Individual flowers are tiny and inconspicuous, as they lack petals, consisting of just two to six stamens and three to four stigmas. The fruits are drupes that contain a single seed.

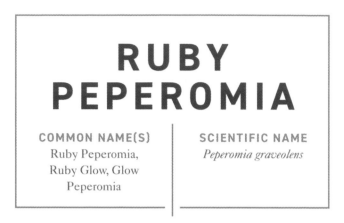

RUBY PEPEROMIA

COMMON NAME(S)
Ruby Peperomia,
Ruby Glow, Glow
Peperomia

SCIENTIFIC NAME
Peperomia graveolens

GENUS ETYMOLOGY: From the Greek words for "pepper" and "resembles" (*pipéri* and *homoios*).

SPECIFIC ETYMOLOGY: From the Latin words for "heavy" and "smelling" (*gravis* and *olens*).

CORE CHARACTERISTICS: An evergreen, mound-forming plant up to 20 cm in height. It features erect, red-colored stems that have thick, bluntly ovate leaves. The leaves are 2–3 cm long and feature an indented, V-shaped, glossy, bluish-green light window across the entire upper surface, making the leaf superficially resemble a canoe overall. The lower surface of the leaves is wine red, with a matte appearance. The red coloration is believed to be an adaptation to absorb light in the green wavelengths, which is reflected upward from forest floor vegetation. The inflorescence is a terminal raceme that bears minute, yellowish-white flowers barely visible to the naked eye. The flowers emit a strong foul fragrance that is reminiscent of mouse urine.

ORIGIN AND HABITAT: It is native to southern Ecuador, only known from two locations. It is found at moderate elevations on Andes mountain cliffs.

PEPPER ELDER

COMMON NAME(S)
Pepper Elder,
Shining Bush Plant,
Man to Man

SCIENTIFIC NAME
Peperomia pellucida

GENUS ETYMOLOGY: From the Greek words for "pepper" and "resembles" (*peperi* and *homoios*).

SPECIFIC ETYMOLOGY: From the Latin word for "transparent" (*pellucidus*).

CORE CHARACTERISTICS: A slender, herbaceous annual or short-lived perennial that can grow up to 45 cm tall but is typically less than 25 cm. The freely branching stems are succulent and brittle. They are mostly erect but occasionally trail and root at the nodes. The fleshy leaves are shiny and glabrous, alternately arranged, broadly ovate or deltate in shape, and up to 4 cm long and 3 cm wide. The plant emits a mustard-like odor when crushed. The inflorescences are loosely flowered spikes that can be terminal, axillary, or opposite the leaves. Individual flowers are tiny and inconspicuous, with whitish or pale green floral parts. The fruit is a globular nutlet that contains a single seed. The nutlets are approximately 0.7 mm in diameter and turn black when ripe, making the flower spike appear to be covered by black dots. Pepper Elder has been used as a food source, a medicinal plant, and an ornamental. Extracts from the plant have been shown to have analgesic, antibacterial, and antifungal properties.

ORIGIN AND HABITAT: It has an extensive native distribution worldwide, including the southern United States to Brazil, central and western Africa, and from India to China to northeastern Australia. It is found in primarily damp, shady habitats.

GLOSSARY

ACAULESCENT: A stemless plant, or one appearing to be stemless.

ACUMINATE: Tapers to a point, such as the tip of a leaf.

ADVENTITIOUS ROOT: Roots that grow from non-root tissues, such as stems or leaves.

AMORPHOUS: Lacking a defined shape or form.

APPRESSED: Lying flat and pressed closely together.

AREOLE: A structure unique to the Cactus family that is essentially a reduced and compressed shoot from which the spines grow. It typically looks like a small, raised disc.

ASCIDIA: A flask-shaped structure or appendage on a plant.

AXIL: The location on a shoot or stem where leaves develop.

BLOOM: A delicate, powdery coating.

BRACTEOLE: A small bract.

BULBIL: A small bulb-like structure produced above ground on a plant for asexual reproduction.

CAUDEX: A short, thickened stem at the base of a plant.

CILIATE: Conspicuous hairs along a leaf margin.

CLADODE: A flattened, leaf-like stem.

COMPOSITE FLOWER: The type of flower present in the Aster (daisy) family, consisting of multiple small, simple flowers that appear to be a single flower.

CORYMB: A flower cluster with a convex or flattened top.

CUNEATE: Wedge-shaped, with a pointed end at the leaf base.

CYME: A type of flower cluster in which the terminal flower develops and opens first, followed by additional flowers developing below it.

DELTOID: A triangular shape, usually with the bottom two corners rounded off.

DICHOTOMOUS: When a shoot or stem branches into two.

DIOECIOUS: When male and female flowers are produced on separate plants.

DISTICHOUS: Leaves arranged in two rows on opposite sides of the stem.

DIVARICATE: When branches diverge at wide angles from each other.

ELLIPTICAL: An oval leaf shape with the widest point at the middle of the leaf, with both ends tapering equally.

ENSIFORM: Sword-shaped.

ENTIRE: A leaf margin that is smooth, lacking teeth or indentations.

EPIPHYTE: A plant that grows on another plant for support.

FARINA: A flour-like mealy coating, usually on leaves.

FASCICLE: A closely-crowded cluster, such as leaves or flowers.

FENESTRATION: A hole, slit, or translucent area on a plant—usually leaves or petals.

FOLLICLE: A dry fruit containing one compartment with at least two seeds and opening along a suture.

FUSIFORM: A leaf shape that resembles a spindle, i.e., is widest in the middle, with both ends tapering to a point.

GEOPHYTE: A plant with an underground water and energy storage structure.

GLABROUS: A hairless, smooth surface.

GLANDULAR HAIR: Hairs on a plant that produce a secretion.

GLAUCOUS: A surface with a blue-to-gray-colored waxy or powdery coating that easily rubs off.

GLOBOSE: Circular.

GLOCHIDIA: Small hair-like spines, often barbed or hooked, that grow from the areoles of some types of cacti.

HERBACEOUS: A plant that lacks woody tissue.

HETEROPHYLLIC: Having different sizes and shapes of leaves on one plant.

IDIOBLAST: A cell that differs in form and function from the surrounding cells.

IMBRICATE: Having overlapping margins, similar to shingles on a roof.

INFLORESCENCE: The complete flowering part (or parts) of a plant.

INTERGENERIC: Occurring between two different genera.

KEEL: Having a ridge-like structure, similar to the bottom of a boat.

LANCEOLATE: A leaf shape that is longer than wide, with a broad base that is wider and tapers to a pointed tip.

LAX: A form or arrangement that is scattered or distant, the opposite of crowded.

LITHOPHYTE: A plant that grows directly in or on solid rock.

MATTE: A surface that is smooth and not shiny.

MONOCARPIC: A plant that flowers and fruits only once in its lifetime, after which it dies.

MUCRONATE: When the tip of a structure (usually a leaf or bract) has a small, sharp point.

MYRMECOPHILOUS: An organism that has an association or relationship with ants.

NODE: The location on a stem or shoot where branches form or a leaf is attached.

NUTLET: A small nut, which is a dry single-seeded fruit.

OBLANCEOLATE: An inversed lanceolate leaf, where the base is the narrower, pointed part.

OBLONG: A leaf shape that is widest in the middle, with two parallel margins.

OVATE/OVOID: A symmetrically curved leaf, with the widest part below the middle, like an egg.

PANICLE: A multibranched cluster of flowers, with each flower attached to a pedicel.

PAPILLATE: A surface with tiny bump-like projections.

PEDICEL: The stalk on which a flower is attached to the central axis or stem of an inflorescence.

PEDUNCLE: The stalk on which an inflorescence is attached to the stem.

PENDANT: A structure that is hanging or suspended.

PLICATE: A structure folded multiple times longitudinally, similar to a fan or corrugated cardboard.

POLLINIA: A cohesive cluster of pollen grains.

PROCUMBENT: A plant that grows horizontally along the ground and does not produce any adventitious roots from its stems.

PROTUBERANCE: Any visibly raised part on the surface of a structure, similar to a swelling or lump.

PRUINOSE: A dusty or powdery frost-like coating on the surface of a structure.

PUBESCENT: A surface covered by short hairs.

RACEME: A type of inflorescence in which the flowers are on short stalks of equal length, equally distant from each other, with the lowest flowers opening first.

RHIZOME: An underground stem that grows horizontally.

SCALLOPED: An edge or margin of a structure with short, rounded teeth.

SEPAL: The outer parts of a flower that enclose and protect it during development.

SPATULATE: A leaf shape broadly rounded at the tip and tapers to a narrow base.

STAMINODE: A rudimentary and sterile stamen, thus not producing pollen. They often appear petal-like and produce nectar.

SUBSHRUB: A small shrub-like plant that is primarily herbaceous, with a woody base.

TENDRIL: A modified stem or leaf that is threadlike and coiled and used by vines for climbing and attachment purposes.

TEPAL: The sepals and petals of a flower when the two are indistinguishable.

TERETE: A structure that is round in cross section and usually tapered and both ends.

TESSELLATED: An appearance characterized by a pattern of repeated shapes that do not overlap and do not have any gaps between them, such as a checkerboard or honeycomb.

TRAILING: A plant with stems that grow along the ground and produce adventitious roots.

TRIGONUS: A structure that is triangular in cross section.

TUBER: A thickened underground stem used for food or water storage by a plant.

TUBERCULE: A round, wart-like projection on the surface of a structure.

UMBEL: A type of inflorescence where a cluster of flower stalks all emerge from the same location, similar to the ribs of an umbrella.

UMBILICATE: A usually circular depression on the surface of a structure, similar to a belly button.

URCEOLATE: A type of flower that is tubular, with a swollen base that narrows to an opening, resembling an urn.

VARIEGATED: A structure with two or more colors in irregularly shaped patterns.

VIVIPAROUS: When the seeds of a plant germinate while still attached to the parent plant.

WHORL: When three or more leaves grow from a single node, usually equidistant from each other around the stem.

ACKNOWLEDGMENTS

We would first like to thank each other, as these books wouldn't have been possible without the love, support, criticism and praise we have directed at each other during the entire writing process. That being said, we would be remiss if we didn't thank our children, Nolan and Anya, for their understanding and patience while we were busy on our computers for hours on end (sometimes), as well as the occasional assist in looking something up for us while we were writing. The editor, Lindy Pokorny, who has been such a delight to work with. The designer, Jordan Stockman, and the illustrator, Vlad Stankovic, who have beautifully turned a bunch of pages with words on them into a work of art. We thank you all!

AUTHOR BIOS

DR. KIT CARLSON earned her PhD in plant microbiology and pathology at the University of Missouri, and conducted her postdoctoral research at Virginia Tech, focused on molecular diagnostics of plant disease. Kit has been a botany professor for nearly two decades. During her tenure, she has served thousands of students and developed and instructed more than 15 different plant science courses. She and her students have conducted and published research on a wide range of topics, including plant disease, medicinal plants, ethnobotany, public land, science education, and more. She is also the author of *The Book of Killer Plants* and coauthor of *Foraging: A Guide to Edible Wild Plants*, *The Book of Invasive Species*, and *How to Keep Your Plants Alive*.

AARON CARLSON is an award-winning naturalist recognized for his contributions to observing rare plant species in their native habitats. Aaron received his BS in biology and wildlife at the University of Wisconsin–Stevens Point, and attended the University of Missouri for his graduate work in limnology. When not working as an educator or lab technician, Aaron spends his free time observing and documenting the life histories of lichens, plants, fungi, and animals. Aaron lives in southern Wisconsin with his wife, their two children, and their poodle. He is also the coauthor of *Foraging: A Guide to Edible Wild Plants*, *The Book of Invasive Species*, and *How to Keep Your Plants Alive*.

ABOUT CIDER MILL PRESS
BOOK PUBLISHERS

Good ideas ripen with time. From seed to harvest, Cider Mill Press brings fine reading, information, and entertainment together between the covers of its creatively crafted books. Our Cider Mill bears fruit twice a year, publishing a new crop of titles each spring and fall.

"Where Good Books Are Ready for Press"

501 Nelson Place
Nashville, Tennessee 37214
cidermillpress.com